Color Library Travel Series

NEW ENGLAND

Designed and Produced by
Ted Smart & David Gibbon

MAYFLOWER BOOKS · NEW YORK CITY

Boston, the cultural, commercial and industrial center of New England, displays with pride both its rich cultural heritage and the products of its progressive planning. Interspersed among its impressive skyline *overleaf* are a wealth of historic buildings including the Massachusetts State House *above left,* and Faneuil Hall *right,* adjacent to the Marketplace *far right.* Part of the plaza adjoining the Christian Science Church Center, seen in the foreground *above,* is shown *left.*

FLOWER GARDEN

SHERATON

Closely associated with the history of New England are the tall-masted ships: the Mayflower II *above,* at Plymouth, and the U.S.S Constitution *left* and Brig Beaver I *right,* at Boston. *Overleaf* is shown a superb aerial view of Boston Common and the city skyline.

Picturesque lighthouses, perched on rocky promontories, such as the Pemaquid Lighthouse overlooking Muscongus Bay *left;* the Bass Harbor Light set in the cliffs of Acadia National Park *above,* and the famous Portland Lighthouse *right,* are often an essential feature on the rugged and spectacular coastline of Maine.

Throughout the seasons New England's charm is all-pervading: in Maine's delightful wooded settings *right;* houses at Wiscasset *below,* and churches, such as that at Bethel *above* which nestles amid the colorful fall foliage. Deepening hues frame the house in Manchester, New Hampshire *left.*

Above left is shown a house in Duxbury, Mass.; *below left* the Rev. Jonathan Ashley House, and *above* the Dwight-Barnard House Museum in Deerfield, Mass.; *right* the Hamilton Laboratory Farm Buildings in Acadia National Park, Maine, and *below and far right* Wiscasset, Maine.

Maine's delightful resort of Boothbay can be seen *above; above and below right* picturesque Menemsha at Martha's Vineyard, Mass.; *below* cod-fishing off Provincetown *left,* at the tip of Cape Cod, and *overleaf* a farm in the countryside near Rutland, Vermont.

POOLE'S FISH

MS 9136 K

The University of Vermont Morgan Horse Farm, with its famous Morgan horses *below,* can be seen *right; above* a tranquil farm near Waterbury, Vermont, and on the *facing page* rural scenes in the re-created New England farming community of Old Sturbridge Village.

24699

ARGONAUT

New England's lovely coastal communities are evidenced in Historic Provincetown, Mass. *above;* Providence *above right,* the capital of Rhode Island, and Boothbay Harbor *left.* Shown *right* is Cape Cod's much photographed Chatham Lighthouse; *below* ripening pumpkins on the lawn of a gracious Rhode Island home, and *overleaf* beautiful Yale University, New Haven, Connecticut.

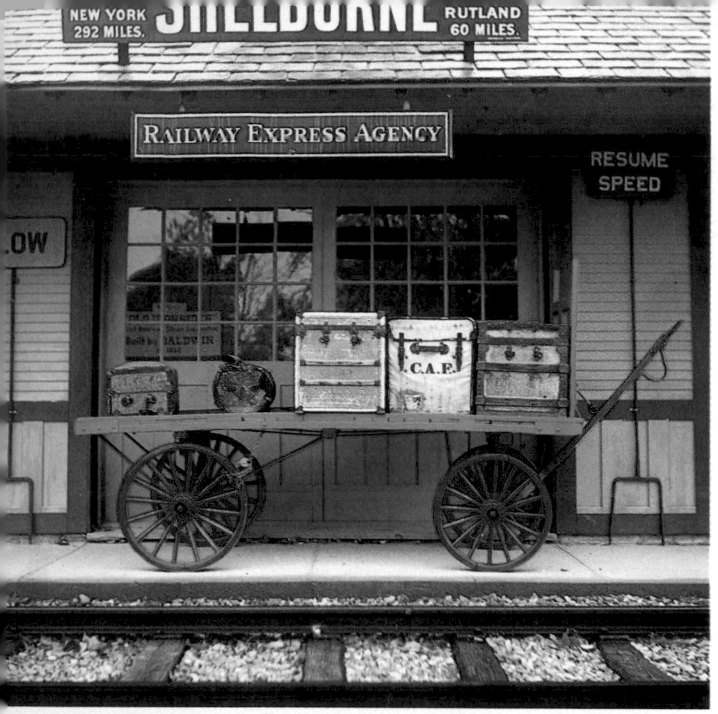

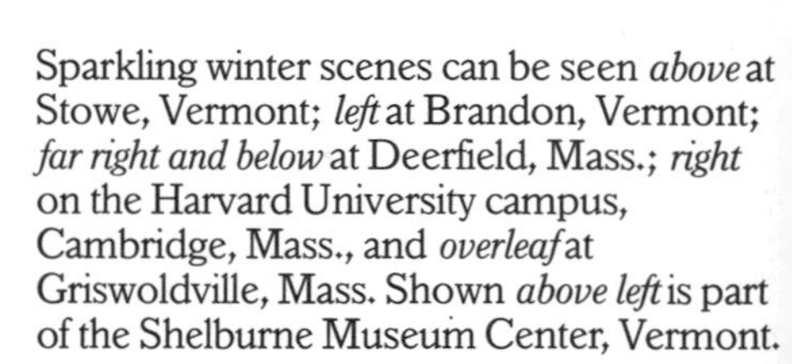

Sparkling winter scenes can be seen *above* at Stowe, Vermont; *left* at Brandon, Vermont; *far right and below* at Deerfield, Mass.; *right* on the Harvard University campus, Cambridge, Mass., and *overleaf* at Griswoldville, Mass. Shown *above left* is part of the Shelburne Museum Center, Vermont.

Little Spruce
DOUBLE CHAIR LIFT
LIFT TICKETS
TOW-AWAY
ZONE